the Girls' Holiday book

Buster Books

Written by Ellen Bailey
Illustrated by Nellie Ryan
Edited by Jen Wainwright
Designed by Zoe Quayle

Cover illustrated by Nikalas Catlow

First published in Great Britain in 2009 by Buster Books,
an imprint of Michael O'Mara Books Limited,
9 Lion Yard, Tremadoc Road, London SW4 7NQ

A CIP catalogue record for this book is available from the British Library.

ISBN: 978-1-906082-64-2

6 8 10 9 7 5

www.mombooks.com/busterbooks

This book was printed in May 2010 by L.E.G.O., Viale dell'Industria 2, 36100, Vicenza, Italy.

CONTENTS

Draw your dream holiday destination.

BORED ON BOARD?

Had enough of playing *I Spy*?
Try out these travel games and time will fly ...

IN MY SUITCASE I HAVE PACKED ...

The first player says, 'In my suitcase I have packed ...', then names an item beginning with A, such as, 'an Alarm clock'.

The second player then says, 'In my suitcase I have packed ...', and then says the previous item, and one of their own that begins with a B, for example, 'an Alarm clock and a Ball'.

The game continues until you have been through the whole alphabet, or until a player forgets one of the items.

CELEBRITY INTERVIEW

Take it in turns to pretend to be a famous person who is being interviewed for a radio programme. The other players must ask you questions and use your answers to guess who you are.

COLOURFUL CARS

Each player picks a colour. The winner is the first to see 30 cars of their chosen colour.

ODD OR EVEN

Each player chooses 'odd' or 'even'. On the count of three, all players raise their hands, each holding up as many fingers as they want.

Count up the total number of fingers raised to find out if it is an odd or an even number. Those who guessed correctly score a point.

FAMILY ACT

Take it in turns to act like one of your holiday companions. The first person to guess who you are pretending to be scores a point and gets to have the next go.

Warning: Make sure no one gets offended – these travel games are supposed to make your journey more fun, not more stressful!

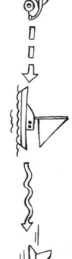

RELAXATION STATION

When you travel, getting stuck in traffic or hanging around at an airport or a station can be a real stress. These simple techniques will keep you and your family feeling relaxed and raring to go.

HEALING HANDS

You can perform this simple hand massage on a friend or family member anywhere – in the car, by the pool, in your bedroom or even in a café. Follow the steps below to pamper and relax your 'client'.

Step One. Ask your client to take off any rings before you start. Hold one of your client's hands palm upwards in both your hands. Your fingers should be underneath, and your thumbs on top. Use your thumbs to apply some pressure and make ten large circles over your client's palm.

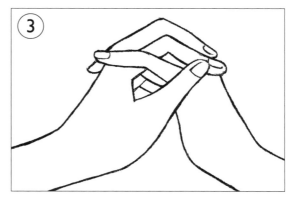

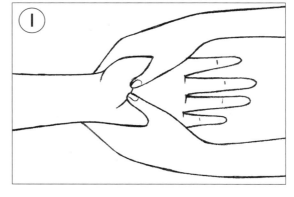

Step Two. Take your client's hand in your left hand. Hold the bottom of their thumb with the thumb and index finger of your right hand. Slide your grip up to the top of their thumb. Gently squeeze the nail, then release. Do this three times and then repeat on each of their fingers.

Step Three. Hold your client's wrist with your left hand, and interlock the fingers of your right hand with theirs, so that your palms are facing. Gently move your client's wrist round in a circle five times, first in one direction and then in the other direction. Finally, repeat step one.

Now begin the complete sequence again on the other hand.

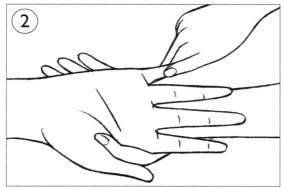

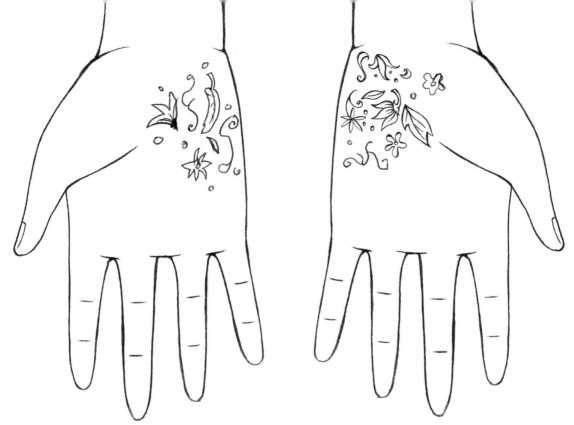

Can you decorate these hands with henna?

JOURNEY YOGA

On a long journey, stay cool and calm with these yoga moves that stretch tired muscles.

Sit with your bottom close to the front of your chair. Take three deep breaths, then perform these two moves.

Sunshine Stretch. Tuck your left foot underneath the chair and slide your right foot forward as far as it will go. Keeping your back straight and your left arm by your side, breathe in as you stretch your right arm up in front of you. Breathe out as you lower your arm, then repeat three times with each arm.

Chair Cat. Sit with your feet flat on the floor and your hands on your thighs. Stretch your body up and backwards so that you're looking at the ceiling, breathing out as you do so.

Now breathe in as you lean forward over your knees and stretch the back of your neck. Repeat five times.

EAGLE EYES

Who'll be the first of your family or friends to spot each of the items below?

Write that person's initials in the box next to the item. The winner is the person who spots the most. You might be able to spot everything listed on a long car journey, or it might take you the whole holiday.

WHAT CAN YOU SPOT?

1. Traffic lights	✓	16. A bakery	
2. A train station		17. A white van	✓
3. Someone wearing red		18. A supermarket	✓
4. A dog		19. A taxi	
5. A police car	✓	20. An aeroplane	
6. A hairdresser's shop		21. A book shop	✓
7. A bus stop	✓	22. A museum	
8. A bridge	✓	23. A washing line	
9. A lorry	✓	24. A convertible car	
10. Someone taking photos		25. Someone using a phone	
11. Someone on roller skates		26. A restaurant	✓
12. A caravan	✓	27. Someone wearing a uniform	✓
13. A baby		28. A cinema	✓
14. Flowers	✓	29. A sweet shop	
15. A phone box		30. A fire engine	

MIND GAMES

These fun games trick the brain and the body.

SAY WHEN

Ask a friend to hold out her arm and close her eyes. Start stroking the inside of her arm just above her wrist, moving up, down and sideways, but gradually heading towards the inside of her elbow. Tell her to shout when she thinks your finger is directly on the dip at the inside of her elbow. You'd be surprised how many people get this wrong.

BILLY GOAT GRUFF

Ask a friend to stand or sit with her back to you. Say 'How many horns does the billy goat have?' At the same time, press some of the fingers of one hand into her back – spread them as widely as you can. Your friend has to guess how many fingers you are using. The best thing about this game is that young people tend to be better at guessing than adults.

THROUGH THE FLOOR

Ask a friend to lie on her back on the floor. Grab her ankles, and lift her feet off the floor until they're level with your waist.

Ask her to shut her eyes and breathe deeply. Hold her legs in this position for one minute, then very slowly lower them towards the ground. Your friend will expect her legs to reach the floor long before they actually do. She will feel as if her legs are passing through the floor!

PUZZLE HOTEL

Complete the puzzles and turn to page 62 to find out the answers.

Can you spot seven differences between these two hotel rooms?

Look at these room keys.
Which two keys are exactly the same?

Can you find your way through the
corridors to the rooftop restaurant?

Which bag belongs to which
family member?

TRAVEL TRIVIA

Test out your family's holiday knowledge with this fun quiz. Use the scorecard opposite to fill in your answers, check to see if they're right on page 62, and find out who is top at travel trivia.

1. In which city would you find the River Seine?

A. Madrid

B. Berlin

C. Paris

D. New York

2. What is special about Italy's tower of Pisa?

A. It's the tallest tower in the world

B. It's leaning over ✓

C. There is a pizza restaurant at the top

D. You can see it from space

3. Which of the following names are you not allowed to call a pig in France.

A. Bill

B. Napoleon

C. Simon

D. Vince

4. In which country would you find the deadly funnel-web spider?

A. Iceland

B. France

C. Australia

D. United Kingdom

5. What would happen if you jumped into Israel's Dead Sea?

A. You'd freeze

B. You'd sink

C. You'd float

D. You'd be surrounded by sharks

6. What is the basic unit of currency in China?

A. Yuan

B. Yan

C. Yen

D. Yin

7. In Chile, it is rude to show someone an open palm with the fingers separated. It means you think they are …

A. Ugly

B. Greedy

C. Lazy

D. Stupid

8. Which of the following isn't one of the Seven Wonders of the Ancient World?

A. The Great Pyramids

B. The Hanging Baskets of Babylon

C. The Temple of Achilles

D. The Statue of Zeus at Olympia

9. What are Niagara Falls?

    A. Waterfalls

    B. Mountains

    C. Pyramids

    D. Oceans

10. Which of these is a beach in Sydney, Australia?

    A. Bondi beach

    B. Mouldy beach

    C. Fungi beach

    D. Tripod beach

11. In which continent is the Amazon Rainforest?

    A. Asia

    B. Africa

    C. South America

    D. Europe

12. In which continent is the South Pole found?

    A. Europe

    B. Antarctica

    C. Africa

    D. North America

Question	Player 1	Player 2	Player 3	Player 4
1				
2				
3				
4				
5				
6				
7				
8				
9				
10				
11				
12				
Total				

PICNIC PERFECTION

Add some glamour when you plan a perfect picnic.

FABULOUS FLOWERS

To make these beautiful folded lotus flowers, all you'll need are some square napkins – it doesn't matter whether they are made of paper or fabric.

1. Open out the napkin and spread it flat. Fold each corner of the napkin into the centre, as shown below. You will now have a small square.

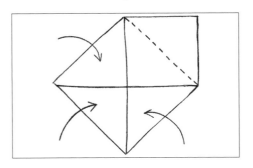

2. Fold each corner of the new square into the centre. You will now have an even smaller square.

3. Turn the napkin over, and again fold each corner into the centre.

4. Hold the centre of the napkin with one hand. Use your other hand to reach underneath the napkin and pick up one of the folded bottom corners.

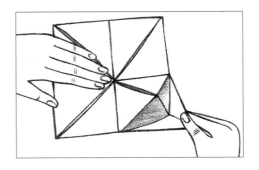

5. Pull the bottom corner up and out to create a petal. You'll need to push the top corner into the middle of the petal. Repeat for each corner.

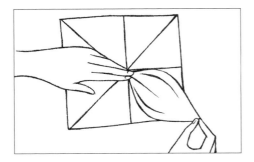

6. You will now have a flower shape. Keeping hold of its centre, reach underneath again and pick up one of the folded-in bottom corners from the inner layer. Pull it up and out to create a smaller petal.

7. Repeat for each of the four folded-in corners. You will now have a beautiful lotus flower.

14

PICNIC PUZZLE

The girls have made a list of some of the food at
their picnic, but two of their items are wrong.

They think that there are:
5 cheese slices, 5 cupcakes, 4 croissants,
6 watermelon slices and 10 strawberries.
How many of each can you see?
Check your answers on page 62.

SURF'S UP!

Everybody's gone surfing. Grab your board and join in with these surf activities.

POP-UP ON YOUR BOARD

Don't let a lack of waves to ride bother you. If you are a true surfer girl, you can perfect a surfing technique called a 'pop-up' whether you're on the beach or in your bedroom. Here's how:

1. Place a towel on the floor and fold it lengthways.

2. Lie on your stomach along the towel, and paddle your arms as though you're swimming your board through the water.

3. When you're ready to catch a wave, place your palms flat on the towel underneath your shoulders. Keeping your body straight, use your arms to do a full push-up, as shown below.

4. Pull your knees towards your stomach, hop onto your feet, and stand up with one foot in front of the other on the 'board'. This is called a 'pop-up'.

The pop-up should be one swift, smooth motion straight to a standing position. So keep practising until you're a super-confident surf chick.

SURFER GIRLS

A. How many girls have bikinis? 5

B. How many have wetsuits? 7

C. How many have only one foot on their board? 2

D. How many have ponytails? 7

Check your answers on page 62.

HOLIDAY HERO

'OK, I'll come, but I'm not getting wet!'

'Just get on the boat, Amrita, and please try and look like you're enjoying yourself,' begged Amrita's mum.

Amrita looked over her shoulder at her friends playing on the beach. It was so unfair! She was terrified of the sea. When she was little she'd been knocked over by a huge wave and banged her head.

Taking care not to look at the waves swelling either side of the boat, she jumped in. Inside there were rows of orange plastic seats and it smelled of fish. This was not her idea of fun.

Other people started to board the boat, laughing and taking photos. Amrita sat down, refusing to look at her mum or her sister, Sophia, as they passed.

The engine started and, with a giant rumble, the boat pulled away. With tears in her eyes Amrita looked out of the back window, and watched as her friends disappeared in the distance.

Half an hour later the boat stopped and there was a great commotion as people rummaged through the boat's supply of flippers, snorkels and masks. Sophia was floating in her rubber ring laughing as a group of children splashed around her.

Amrita moved to the other side of the boat so that she wouldn't have to see everyone having fun without her. She saw a young boy wearing a rubber ring in the water. She realised he was being dragged away from the boat by the current. He was crying and waving his arms. Amrita knew that she had to get help before he disappeared out of sight, but there was no-one else on the boat.

'Help,' she cried, but no-one could hear her. She rushed out onto the deck. 'It's OK,' she called to the boy. 'I'm coming.'

Amrita's heart was pounding, but she didn't have time to think. She jumped in fully clothed. Everything she'd learnt at swimming lessons came rushing back to her, and she swam towards the boy.

'Are you alright?' she shouted to him when she got close, but the boy just kept crying. Quickly, she began to pull him by the rubber ring back towards the boat, but it was really hard work.

She saw that a crowd had gathered on the boat, and people were swimming towards her. A man got there first.

'Thank you, thank you,' he said, as he took the boy from Amrita. 'This is my son, and no-one knew what had happened to him. He just disappeared.'

When they arrived back at the boat everyone was cheering and clapping.

'You're a hero, Amrita,' said her mum. 'I'm so proud of you – I bet you can't wait to tell your friends all about it.'

WRITE TO ME

Fill in your details on these cards. Cut them out and give them
to the friends you make on holiday, so you never lose touch.

Name: Zula
Address: 32 Manse
Rd Cults Aberdeen
Email: Z3born@gmail.com

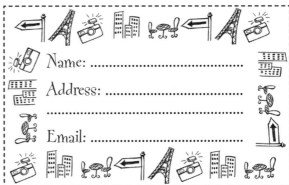

Name: ....
Address: ....
....
Email: ....

Name: ....
Address: ....
....
Email: ....

Name: ....
Address: ....
....
Email: ....

Name: ....
Address: ....
....
Email: ....

Name: ....
Address: ....
....
Email: ....

Colour in each card
before you give it away.

CRACK THOSE CODES

You find these bottles washed up on the beach. Three of them contain riddles written in secret codes, and the fourth contains cryptic clues that will help you crack the codes.

Match each clue to the correct bottle, decipher the messages, then figure out the answers to the riddles. (Answers on pages 62 and 63.)

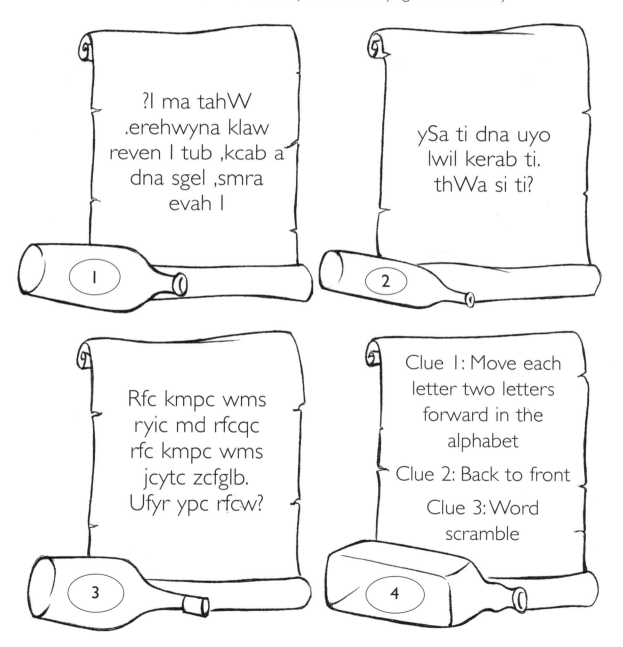

1
?I ma tahW
.erehwyna klaw
reven I tub ,kcab a
dna sgel ,smra
evah I

2
ySa ti dna uyo
lwil kerab ti.
thWa si ti?

3
Rfc kmpc wms
ryic md rfcqc
rfc kmpc wms
jcytc zcfglb.
Ufyr ypc rfcw?

4
Clue 1: Move each
letter two letters
forward in the
alphabet

Clue 2: Back to front

Clue 3: Word
scramble

RAINY-DAY DECISIONS

Don't let the rain get you down. This fortune finder contains loads of great ideas for how to fill the time if you're stuck inside.

HOW TO MAKE IT

1. Cut around the fortune finder on the opposite page. Fold one corner over to the other to make a triangle, so that the writing is on the outside.

2. Fold your triangle in half again to form a smaller triangle. Then unfold the sheet and lie it flat.

4. Turn the fortune finder over and repeat step 3, folding the new corners into the middle.

5. Fold the fortune finder in half from edge to edge, so the colours remain on the outside.

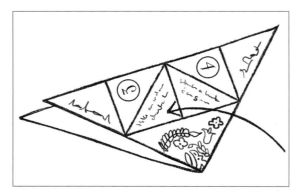

3. Fold each corner of the sheet into the middle, so the corners all meet at the centre of the sheet.

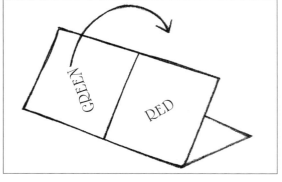

6. Unfold and fold in half the other way.

7. Slide the thumbs and forefinger of both hands under the flaps of the fortune finder, and find your fortune!

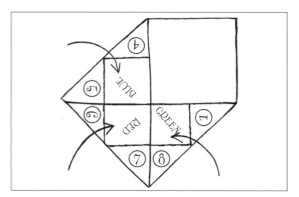

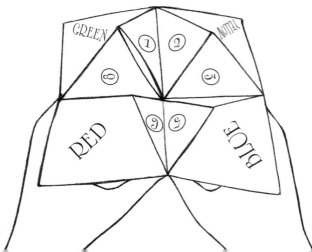

22

HOLIDAY STYLE QUIZ

Everyone looks forward to different things about going on holiday.
Take this quiz and find out what kind of holiday-maker you are.
Find out what your answers mean on the next page.

1. If you could take only one item on holiday with you, what would it be?

- **A.** Magazines
- **B.** Camera
- **C.** Sunglasses
- **D.** Beach ball

4. Which type of shoes do you spend most of your holiday wearing?

- **A.** Flip-flops
- **B.** Sandals
- **C.** High heels
- **D.** Trainers

2. Which item of clothing would you be most annoyed to forget?

- **A.** Sarong
- **B.** Favourite T-shirt
- **C.** Expensive new skirt
- **D.** Swimming costume

5. What is your favourite holiday drink?

- **A.** Milkshake
- **B.** Bottled water
- **C.** Fruit smoothie
- **D.** Energy drink

3. What is the first thing you do when you arrive at your destination?

- **A.** Get an ice cream
- **B.** Flick through a guidebook
- **C.** Hit the local shops
- **D.** Go swimming

6. How will you spend the last day of your holiday?

- **A.** Relaxing on a sun lounger
- **B.** Dashing round all the sights you haven't seen yet
- **C.** At the theatre
- **D.** Playing football with a new group of friends

WHAT YOUR ANSWERS MEAN

Count up how many times you chose each letter and then look at the results below to find out what your answers say about you. If you got an even mix of letters, then you're a girl who likes to try a bit of everything on holiday.

MOSTLY A: LAID-BACK LADY

When you're on holiday, your aim is to kick back and relax. You love lounging by the pool, indulging in long, lazy lunches, and flicking through magazines.

A week or two of this will leave you feeling totally chilled, but make sure you don't miss out on the fun because you've fallen asleep!

MOSTLY C: CITY STAR

You're a sophisticated girl who enjoys visiting new cities and getting to grips with the culture. You always look super-stylish, and love shopping and dining in posh restaurants.

Don't forget that even the most glamorous of girls need some down time, so make sure you leave time to pull on some comfy clothes and unwind.

MOSTLY B: SASSY SIGHTSEER

You're never seen without your camera, and love visiting famous landmarks. The more you can find out about your destination before you go, the more you'll get out of it. So grab that guidebook and get investigating.

MOSTLY D: ACTIVE ADVENTURER

Always the first to suggest a game of beach volleyball or Frisbee, you're a sporty chick who loves to keep active.

Exercise is a great way to relax and have fun on holiday, and will help keep you fit and healthy, too.

 # SCARY STORY TIME

This is the perfect story to tell while sitting round a glowing campfire.

Read it through again and again until you know it by heart, then tell it to your friends on a dark, spooky night. Set the mood by shining a torch under your chin. When you get to the last sentence, whisper the words written in *italics*, then shout the word written in CAPITALS, and watch your friends jump out of their skins!

Did you hear the story that's been in the news about three girls from around here? They'd been out for the day and were heading home when they got caught in a storm. Without any warning, the wind began to howl and lightning flashed across the sky.

They ran up to a house and went to knock on the door, but saw that it was already open. It looked dark and scary inside, but there was no other shelter and they couldn't stay out in the storm, so they went in.

The house was deserted. It was dusty, cold and damp. Scared and wet, the girls huddled together in a corner. They could hear the rain hammering against the windows, and the wind was screeching through the house.

'What's that noise?' asked one of the girls.

'It's just the wind.'

'No, listen…'

Boom, shhhhhhh. Boom, shhhhhhh. Boom, shhhhhhh.

The sound was getting louder.

Boom, shhhhhhh. Boom, shhhhhhh. Boom, shhhhhhh.

Whatever the sound was, it was coming towards them. The girls put their arms round each other, their hearts beating fast in terror.

Boom, shhhhhhh. Boom, shhhhhhh. Boom, shhhhhhh.

There was something standing in the dark right next to them. They heard a voice:

'Don't worry, I'm only a little girl. But I've got a wooden **LEG!***'*

FREAKY FOOD

People around the world have different ideas about what makes a tasty treat.

Can you guess which of the strange snacks below is eaten in which country?
Draw lines to match them up, and check your answers on page 63.
The first one has been done for you.

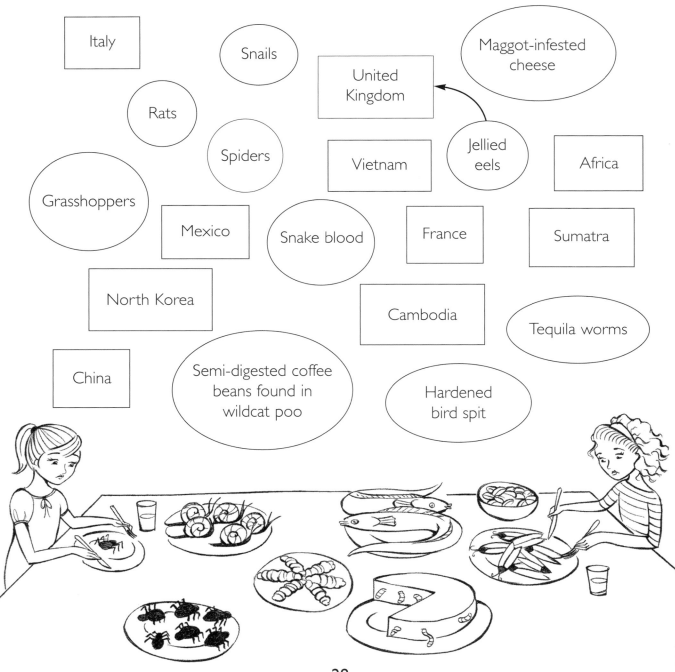

Italy

Snails

United Kingdom

Maggot-infested cheese

Rats

Spiders

Vietnam

Jellied eels

Africa

Grasshoppers

Mexico

Snake blood

France

Sumatra

North Korea

Cambodia

Tequila worms

China

Semi-digested coffee beans found in wildcat poo

Hardened bird spit

PERFECT POSTCARDS

This alternative to a diary is the perfect way to keep a record of everything that happens during your holiday.

1. Buy a postcard each day of your holiday that reminds you of something that happened, or somewhere you went during the day.

2. Every evening, write a diary entry on the back of the day's postcard. Describe where you went and what you saw. You could get your holiday companions to add their comments, too.

3. When you get back from holiday, hole punch each postcard in the top left-hand corner. Make sure that you hole punch each one in the same place so that they line up properly.

4. Thread a piece of ribbon through each of the holes, and tie it in a bow at the top. You will now have a postcard book of holiday memories that will last a lifetime.

HIT THE SLOPES

Race for the finish line with this snowy ski game.

Place a coin for each player by the START line. Then ski down the mountain, keeping an eye out for sneaky shortcuts, or traps that could slow you down. The first one to the FINISH is the winner.

START

A bear is chasing you. Roll again to get away.

You spot an off-piste shortcut. Jump ahead.

There's a blizzard. Miss a turn while you wait for it to pass.

You hitch a ride on a sledge. Take the shortcut.

You crash into another skier. Move back 2 spaces.

You learn a new trick. Roll a 6 to master it and win.

FINISH

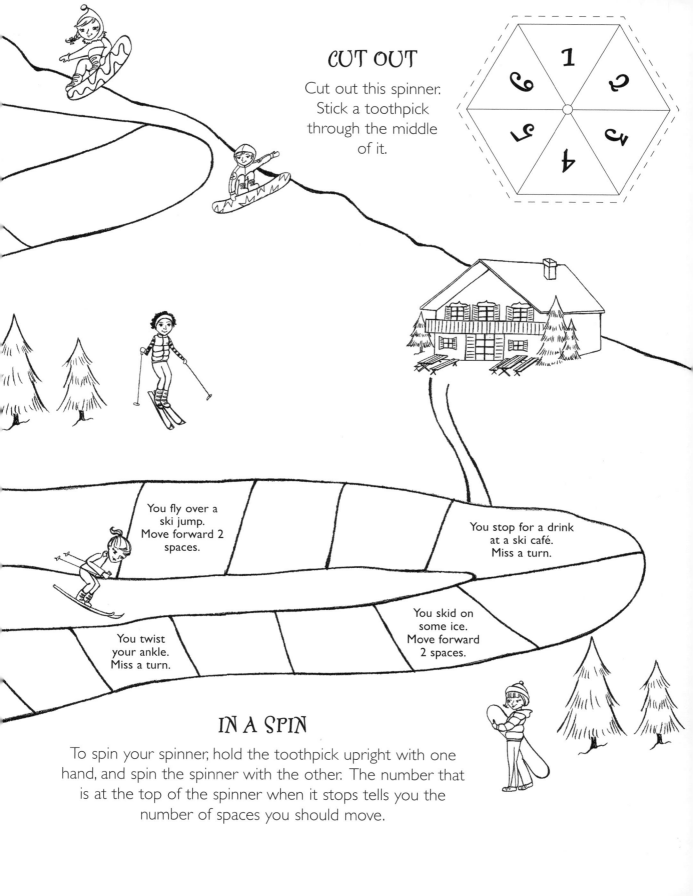

CUT OUT

Cut out this spinner. Stick a toothpick through the middle of it.

1 2 3 4 5 6

You fly over a ski jump. Move forward 2 spaces.

You stop for a drink at a ski café. Miss a turn.

You skid on some ice. Move forward 2 spaces.

You twist your ankle. Miss a turn.

IN A SPIN

To spin your spinner, hold the toothpick upright with one hand, and spin the spinner with the other. The number that is at the top of the spinner when it stops tells you the number of spaces you should move.

What can you see from your window?

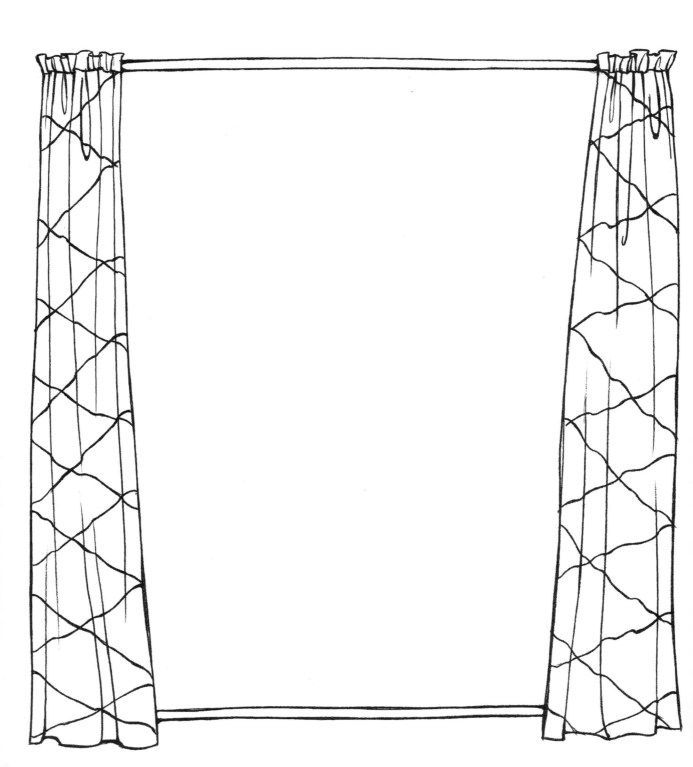

SPEAK UP

Wherever you are in the world, you'll meet holiday-makers from different countries. Become a true international jet-setter by learning to say, 'Hello, my name is …' and, 'Have a good holiday' in several different languages.

A guide to how to pronounce the words is given in *italics* below.

SPANISH

Hola, me llamo …
Ola, mee yammo …

¡Buenas vacaciones!
Bwenas vacatheeohnays!

ITALIAN

Buongiorno, mi chiamo …
Bwonjorno, mee kyamo …

Buona vacanza!
Bwona vacanza!

HINDUSTANI

Namaste, merās nām … ha
Nam-a-stay, merah nam … hi

Śubh yātrā!
Sub yah-trah !

FRENCH

Bonjour, je m'appelle …
Bonjhoor, jhuh mahpehl …

Bonnes vacances!
Bon vahkons!

GERMAN

Guten tag, ich heiße …
Gooten tahg, ick hi-ser …

Schöne Ferien!
Sherne ferry-en!

PORTUGUESE

Olá, meu nome é …
Ola, meeyoo nomeh eh …

Desejo-lhe umas
boas férias!
*Desayjo le oohmas
bo-as fairy-as!*

MANDARIN CHINESE

Nǐhǎo, wǒ jiào …
Neehaw, waw jow …

Yí lù píng ān!
Ee loo ping an!

TURKISH

Merhaba, benim adim …
Mehr-hah-bah, benim adim …

Güle güle!
Gew-leh, gew-leh!

RUSSIAN

Zdravstvujte, men'a
zovut …
*Zdra-stoy-chye, meen-ya
zavoot …*

Sčastlivogo puti!
Shess-lee-vovo pootey!

WATER WORLD

Complete the puzzles and turn to page 63 to check your answers.

Which swimmer will come out of which flume?

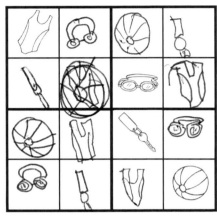

Complete the grid above so that each column, each row, and each of the four larger squares contains only one swimsuit, a beach ball, a locker key and some goggles.

① A ② b ③ C ④ D

Using only three straight lines, divide the swimming pool into six sections, with one swimmer and one beach ball in each.

Can you spot two identical burgers in this diner?

Can you find a clear path for this girl through the maze to the jacuzzi?

35

LUXURY LUGGAGE

Make sure your luggage is instantly recognisable and the most stylish in town with this fabulous oversized luggage tag.

1. Cut a large rectangle (that measures about half the size of this page) from a thick piece of card (an old cereal packet will do). Cut off the top and bottom corners of one side to make your tag shape. Use the point of a pencil to make a hole at one end of it – this will be the hole through which you can thread a ribbon to tie it to your bag.

2. Cut out enough paper to cover one side of your tag, and stick it on with glue. Write your name, postcode and telephone number on it. This means that if your luggage gets lost the person who finds it will be able to return it to you. You could decorate this side with felt-tip pens, and maybe even some glitter or sequins to make it really eye-catching.

3. During your holiday, collect paper souvenirs from your trip, such as ticket stubs, museum brochures, information pamphlets, postcards, sketches, maps, menus, interesting food packaging and stickers. Sort through the items you have collected and cut out pictures or words that look good and remind you of your holiday.

4. Cover the reverse side of your luggage tag with white PVA glue (dilute the glue with water if it's very thick). Stick the pictures on, then cover them with another thick layer of glue.

5. When the glue has dried and the surface of your tag looks shiny, thread a piece of brightly-coloured ribbon or string through the hole and tie it on to the handle of your bag.

SPOT THE FASHIONISTAS

Can you find the two girls below in the crowd?
Answers on page 63.

H   K

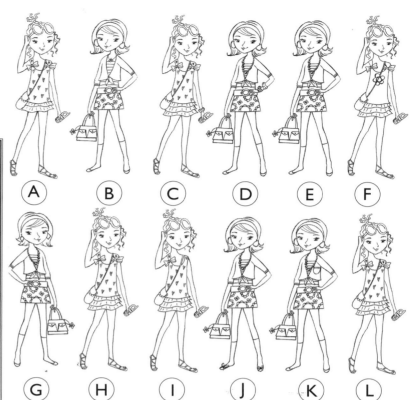

A   B   C   D   E   F

G   H   I   J   K   L

Decorate these flip-flops.

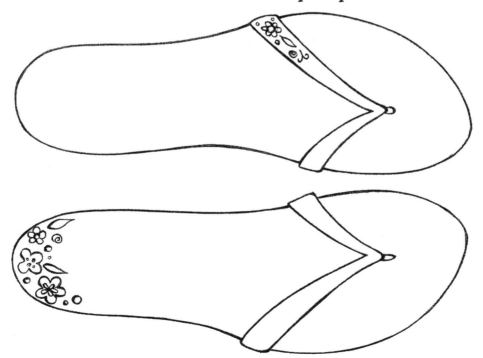

PICTURE THIS

Using the grid lines to help you, draw your own version of this picture in the bigger grid below.

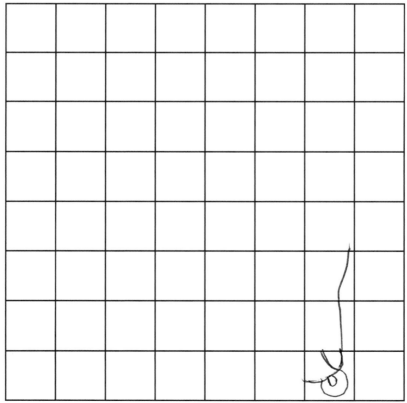

MAP MAYHEM

In map reading, combinations of letters and numbers are known as co-ordinates and refer to locations on the map. To use a co-ordinate, place your finger on the number given. Trace your finger along the row to the column that matches the letter. In that square you will find the symbol that the co-ordinates refer to.

Can you find the symbols at the following co-ordinates and use the key to find out what they mean? Check your answers on page 63.

1. 5A　　**2.** 4E　　**3.** 1F　　**4.** 3B　　**5.** 6D　　**6.** 3G

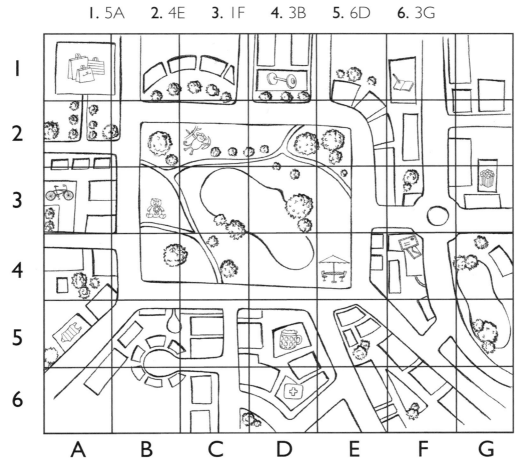

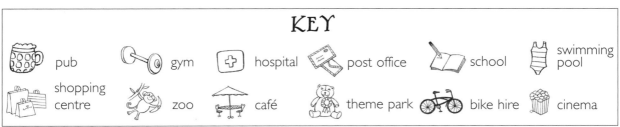

KEY

pub　　gym　　hospital　　post office　　school　　swimming pool

shopping centre　　zoo　　café　　theme park　　bike hire　　cinema

TREASURE HUNT

Look out for the following items while you're on holiday, and stick them in when you find them.

Try to find everything before it's time for you to go home.

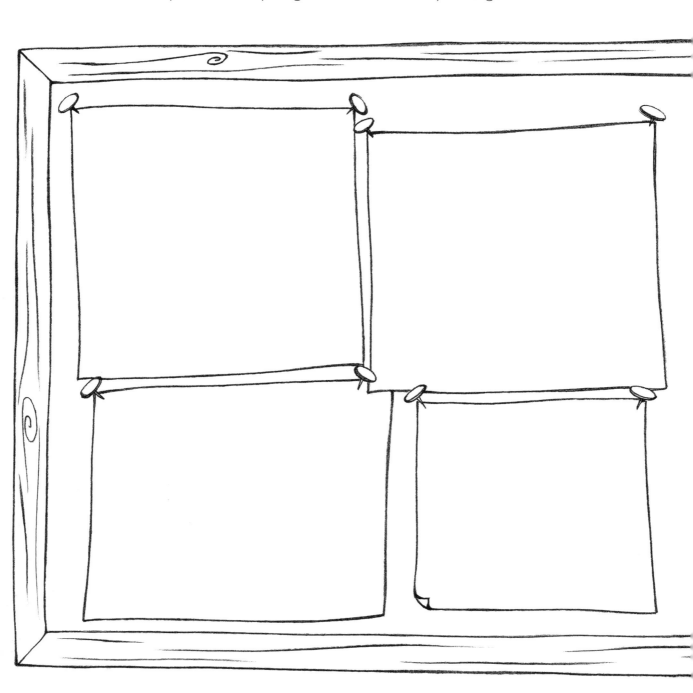

1. A picture of somewhere you visited cut out from a brochure or leaflet.

2. A section of a map that shows where you are staying.

3. A ticket from a journey you went on.

4. A stamp from the country you're in.

5. A napkin from a café or restaurant.

6. A price tag or sticker.

7. The wrapper of a sweet you've never tried before.

8. The smallest coin available in the country you're in.

BEACH BEAUTY

You're armed with your towel, shades, sunscreen and snorkel.
You're ready to have a splashing time at the seaside,
but a girl has her image to think of. So follow these handy hints
to be a beautiful beach babe.

SUMMER HAIR

Fun on the beach can be a nightmare for your hair – the sun and sea water will dry it out.

Keep your locks feeling silky and fight the frizz, by slicking lots of leave-in conditioner on to your hair and comb it through. If your hair is long enough, pull it into a ponytail for extra protection.

Everyone knows sunscreen is essential for anyone venturing out in the sun, but there's nothing worse than a red, sunburnt parting. Always keep the top of your head protected with a hat. Alternatively, tie a headscarf, with the ends behind your head for a super-stylish coverup.

SURFER STYLE

Surfer girls' hair always looks beautifully messy, 'tousled' by fun in the sun, sea and sand.

If you don't get to the beach, you can get the surfer-girl-hair look by mixing two tablespoons of salt in half a litre of warm water. Pour it over your hair after shampooing and don't rinse it out. This salty rinse will give your hair a cool beach-babe look.

WORKING THE WAVES

If it is long enough, wear your hair in plaits all day at the beach. In the evening brush your hair loose for soft, glamorous waves.

SUMMER FEET

Summer is the time to be bold, so paint your toenails with some bright polish.

Why not try painting each nail a different shade? Or, for a truly eye-catching look, use a dark colour first and then add a stripe of a different colour down the middle of each nail.

For super-soft summer feet, put on lots of moisturiser all over your feet before bedtime. Pop on a pair of old socks to protect your bed covers. This helps to keep moisture locked in to the skin of your feet, making them extra soft.

Getting sand between your toes can be annoying, but walking barefoot on the beach rubs away dead skin, leaving the soles of your feet feeling lovely and smooth.

SAND-CASTLE SURPRISE

Everyone wants to be queen of the castle, but this page will make sure it's you who wears the crown, with the best sand castle on the beach.

1. The perfect spot. Choose a site close enough to the sea so that you can easily get water, but not so close that your masterpiece will get washed away. Look for the point where the dark, wet sand starts to turn lighter.

2. Prepare the area. Pour buckets of water onto your chosen area and stamp down the sand until you have a firm area large enough for your sand castle.

3. Build a base. Build up a large mound of wet sand with a flat top. Pat down the sand as you build up the mound to create a firm, flat base for your sand castle.

4. Make the castle. Did you know that there's a scientific formula for building the perfect sand castle? Scientists have found that the winning recipe is $0.125 \times S = OW$, which basically means

Complete this sand castle.

that you should mix one bucket of water with eight buckets of sand to create the perfect sand mixture. Fill your buckets with the mixture, pat the sand down with your spade so that it's flat and compact, then carefully tip over the buckets on top of the mound. One large castle in the middle with four smaller 'turret' sand castles around it looks particularly impressive.

5. Make a moat and castle wall. A moat is a deep trench filled with water that's built around a castle to protect it from attack. Dig out the sand at the base of your sand castle mound to create a trench that goes all the way around it.

Use the sand you've dug out to build up a wall around the outside of the trench. The wall should be about as tall as your hand and as wide as your wrist.

6. Fill the moat with water. Create a trench that goes from the sea to your moat. Start by creating a passageway through the castle wall for the water to pass through. To do this, use your finger to carefully cut an arch into the area of the wall facing the sea. Next, dig a deep trench all the way from the archway to the sea. The sea water will rush down the trench towards your sand castle and fill the moat, guarding it from invaders and protecting your castle.

TREASURE ISLAND

Ahoy there! Head to the treasure island for some puzzle and doodle fun.

A girl is on an island with her mean brother and greedy sister, and a sack of sweets. She needs to get herself, her brother and her sister back to the mainland with the sweets. The raft she has is only large enough to carry her and one thing she needs to take with her, so she will need to make several trips.

The problem is, she can't leave her brother alone with her sister, as he will tease her. She can't leave her sister alone with the sweets, as she will eat them all. Her brother will not eat the sweets, so he can be left alone with them.

Can you work out what she can do? (Answer on page 64.)

What would you take to a desert island?

BEACH SUDOKU

Complete the grid so that each column, each row, and each of the four larger squares contains only one bucket, a spade, a sand castle and an ice cream.

(Answer on page 64.)

Fill the chest with treasure.

47

DESTINATION DETECTIVES

Use your detective skills to search for clues about your holiday destination that will help you answer the questions below.

Even if you're holidaying close to home you might find out some things you didn't know before. Wow your holiday companions with the fascinating facts you've found out, and impress the locals with how much you know about their culture.

What does the country's flag look like? Draw it here.

Draw a piece of art that you saw on holiday.

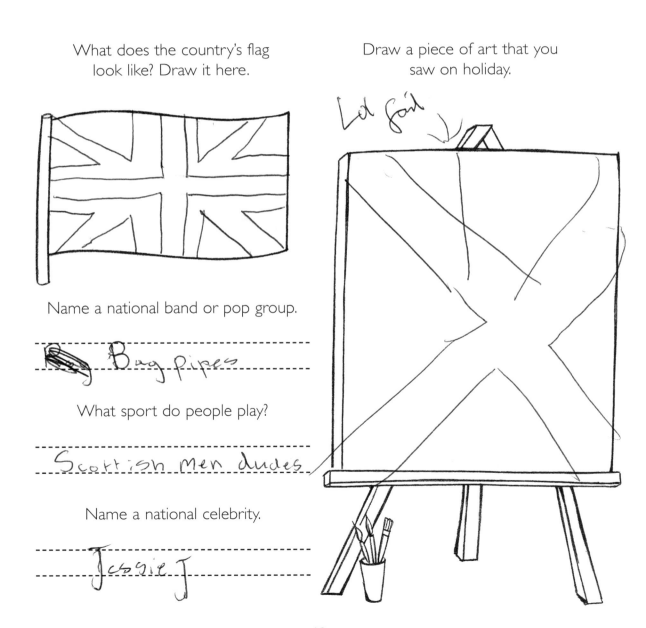

Lol fail

Name a national band or pop group.

Bag pipes

What sport do people play?

Scottish Men dudes

Name a national celebrity.

Jessie J

Who is the leader of the country you're in?

Queen Elisabeth

What currency is used?

Pounds

What does the national dress look like?

Find out the name of a festival that people celebrate in the country.

Christmas

Draw a picture of the local dish.

Pizza!

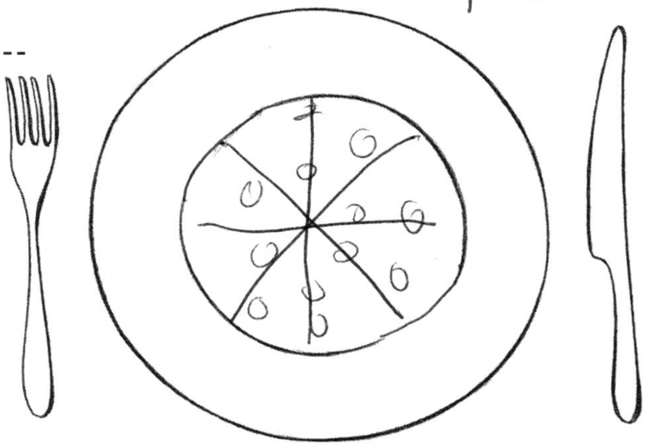

Yum

List three tourist attractions you'd like to visit in the country.

Landmark

Cadenas

What is the biggest difference between the place you are on holiday and home?

good weather

CAMPFIRE TWISTS

It's time to get cooking by the campfire.

These delicious treats are perfect to bake over a campfire. You don't need to measure out the ingredients, and you don't even need any cooking utensils.

1. Make a pile of flour and scoop out the centre to form a well.

2. Pour a little water into the well, and mix together with your hands until you have a lump of dough. Don't worry if it gets messy. Add more flour or water if you need to.

3. Shape the dough with your hands into a large square.

4. Sprinkle lots of chocolate chips onto the middle of the dough, then fold it so that all the chocolate chips are on the inside.

5. Roll out the dough into a long sausage shape.

6. Twist the dough around a skewer or stick and toast over the glowing embers of your campfire.

PHOTO FRENZY

Can you work out which parent took each of the photos below?

You need to think about where each one is standing, and which girl they are aiming their camera at. You'll find the answers on page 64.

SHOP 'TIL YOU DROP

Complete the puzzles and turn to page 64 to check your answers.

You have 300 cents (c) in your purse. If you were going to use all of your money to buy one type of sweet, how many of each type could you buy?

Can you find the sunglasses that match the ones pictured in the magazine above?

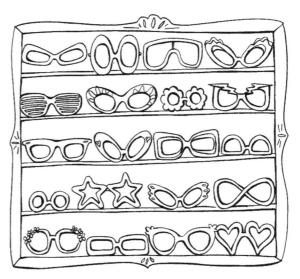

Can you spot 11 differences between the two window displays on the opposite page?

HOLIDAY BINGO

This is a great game that you can play anywhere – on a long journey, on a rainy day or at the beach.

Holiday Bingo is a game for three players. Find out how to play below, then cut out the boards and counters on the next page and you're ready for some bingo fun.

1. You are all going on holiday together, but one player has lost their suitcase and needs to borrow items from the other two. Choose which of you will be the 'suitcase' players and who will be the 'lost luggage' player.

2. Cut out the suitcase game boards and each of the counters. The two 'suitcase' players then choose either the suitcase and counters with the hearts, or the ones with the flowers. (See page 56.)

3. Without letting the 'lost luggage' player see, the two 'suitcase' players

choose six of their counters and place them all face-up on their suitcase game boards.

4. The 'lost luggage' player then calls out in a random order the items from the list below that they would like to borrow.

5. Each time the 'lost luggage' player says the name of an item that one of the 'suitcase' players has on their game board, that player hands the matching counter to the 'lost luggage' player. The winner is the first player to hand over all the items that are on their suitcase game board.

LIST OF ITEMS

1. Travel sweets	7. Sunglasses
2. T-shirt	8. Magazine
3. Towel	9. Day bag
4. Camera	10. Money
5. Toothpaste	11. Hat
6. Hairbrush	12. Travel pillow

55

BAGS OF DIFFERENCE

Oh no! Your bag has been mixed up with someone else's at the airport.
Can you spot five differences between your bag (A) and the other bag?
Answers on page 64.

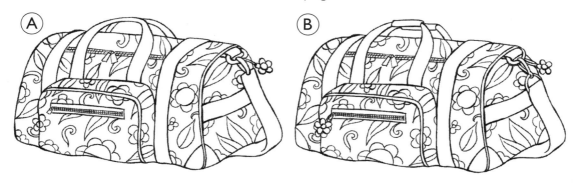

What have you packed in your suitcase?   Yes

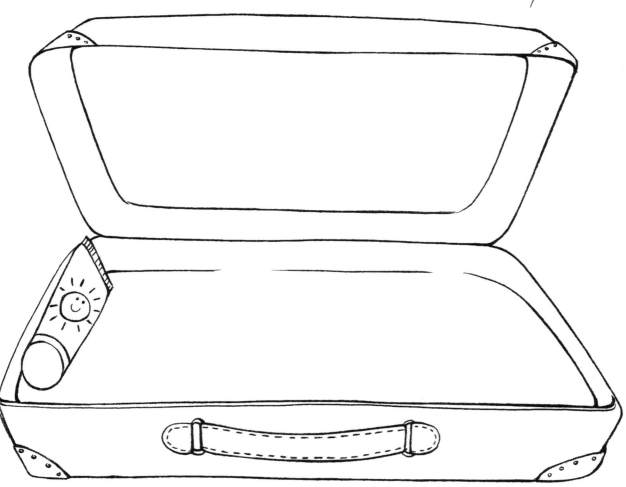

HOLIDAY HIGHLIGHTS

You'll want to remember your holiday forever, so answer these
questions at the end of your trip and keep a record of the highlights.

Holiday Destination: ...... Glasgow ......

Dates – From: Sat. To: Sun.

Who went with you?

Mum Dad brother

Describe the place where you were staying.

Glasgow

What was your favourite holiday activity?

Playing tennis

What was the funniest thing that happened?

I won a gam

If you could re-live one day of your holiday, which would it be?

losing a game

What was the most delicious thing you ate?

Burgur King

58

What was your favourite
holiday outfit?

Was there anything that you did for
the first time during your holiday?

Tennis clothes

Nope

What will you miss most now
you're back at home?

Did you make any new friends?
What are they like?

Nothing Much

None

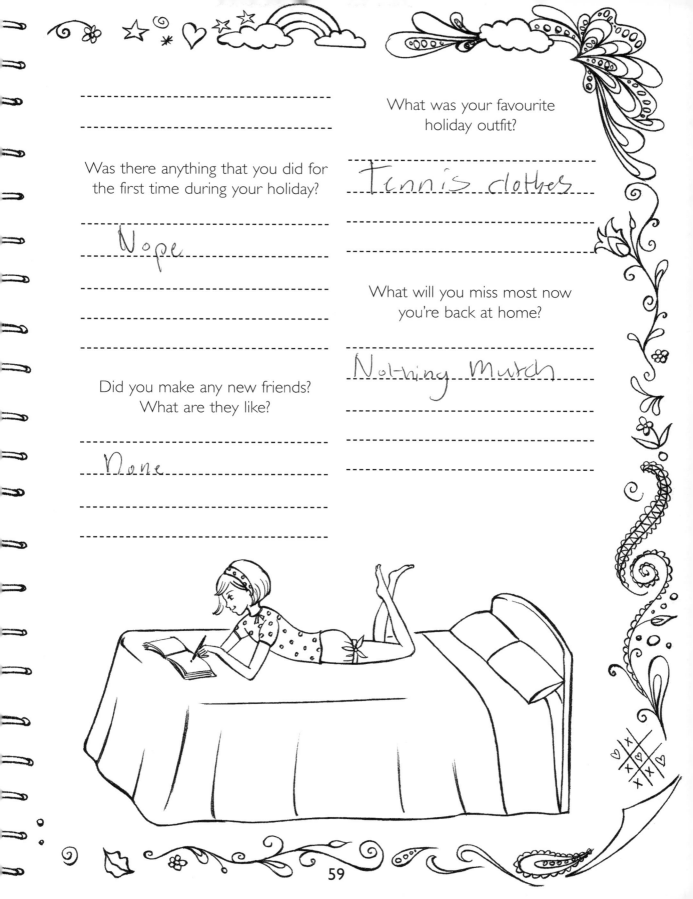

Fill these photo frames with your favourite holiday memories.

ALL THE ANSWERS

PUZZLE HOTEL
pages 10 and 11

Room keys C and L are identical.

Person 1 has bag A.
Person 2 has bag C.
Person 3 has bag D.
Person 4 has bag B.

TRAVEL TRIVIA
pages 12 and 13

1. **C**,   2. **B**,   3. **B**,   4. **C**,

5. **C**,   6. **A**,   7. **D**,   8. **B**,

9. **A**,   10. **A**,   11. **C**,   12. **B**.

PICNIC PUZZLE
page 15

11 Strawberries
6 Cupcakes

SURFER GIRLS
page 17

A. five,   **B.** seven,   **C.** two,   **D.** seven.

CRACK THOSE CODES
page 21

Bottle 1 use clue 2:
Riddle: 'I have arms, legs and a back, but
I never walk anywhere.
What am I?'
Answer: I am a chair.

Bottle 2 use clue 3:
Riddle: 'Say it and you will break it.
What is it?'
Answer: Silence.

Bottle 3 use clue 1:

Riddle: 'The more you take of these the more you leave behind.
What are they?'
Answer: Footsteps.

FREAKY FOOD
page 28

The following foods are eaten in the following countries:

Maggoty cheese in Italy; snake blood in Vietnam; tequila worms in Mexico; snails in France; digested coffee in Sumatra; rats in North Korea; spiders in Cambodia; jellied eels in the United Kingdom; bird spit in China; grasshoppers in Africa.

WATER WORLD
pages 34 and 35

Swimmer A reaches flume 1.
Swimmer B reaches flume 2.
Swimmer C reaches flume 3.
Swimmer D reaches flume 4.

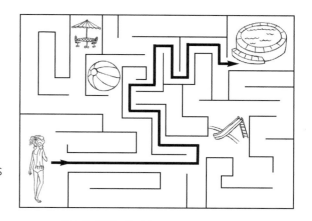

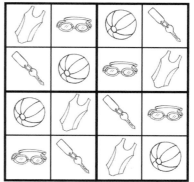

SPOT THE FASHIONISTAS
page 37

The matching girls are E and H.

MAP MAYHEM
page 39

5A is a swimming pool.
4E is a café.
1F is a school.
3B is a theme park.
6D is a hospital.
3G is a cinema.

TREASURE ISLAND
page 46

The girl takes the sister across to the mainland, leaving the brother and the sweets. She returns to the island, and takes her brother to the mainland. Then she takes her sister back to the island with her – so that her brother and sister aren't left alone together.

Next, she leaves her sister on the island, takes the sweets across to the mainland and leaves them with her brother. Finally, she returns to the island and takes her sister back to the mainland.

BEACH SUDOKU
page 47

PHOTO FRENZY
page 51

A 2, B 4, C 5,
D 1, E 3, F 6.

SHOP 'TIL YOU DROP
pages 52 and 53

In the sweet shop you could buy:
17 cola bottles with 11c left over,
6 bonbons, 30 humbugs, 15 toffees,
9 lollipops with 3c left over,
5 liquorices, 3 candy canes with 45c left over, 12 sugar mice,
6 sherbet lemons with 30c left over.

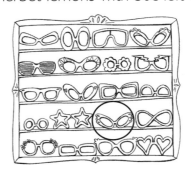

BAGS OF DIFFERENCE
page 57